Hafsah Aneela Bashir is a writer, playwright and performance poet based in Manchester. Her work has been published in anthologies, *When Saira Met Sarah*, *80 Decibels Above Sound*, *Elevator Fiction* and *Shots In The Dark* by Crocus Books.

She is founder and co-director of Outside The Frame Arts (OTFA), a collective platforming marginalised voices. She is currently The Royal Exchange Manchester's Supported Artist 2018-19, Longsight's Writer In Residence with Manchester Literature Festival and a 'Leader of Tomorrow' on the Artistic Directors Leadership Programme.

A former TOAST16 Poet, she has written and performed at HOME Manchester for PUSH Festival 2019 with OTFA's successful *Cuts Of The Cloth*.

She was recently awarded the prestigious Jerwood Compton Poetry Fellowship 2019, has performed for numerous festivals, is creating theatre work of her own exploring womanhood and heritage and is still a sane mother of five.

She tweets at @Hafsah_A_Bashir and @artsOTF.

Burning Eye

BurningEyeBooks
Never Knowingly
Mainstream

This edition published by Burning Eye Books 2018

www.burningeye.co.uk

@burningeyebooks

Burning Eye Books
15 West Hill, Portishead, BS20 6LG

ISBN 978-1-911570-50-9

the
celox
and the
clot

For Mariyah
Idreece
Ismaeel
Isshaaq
Ilyaas

CONTENTS

INTRO

CUMIN SEEDS

A bangled tight grip on my hand
and you take me through suspended plastic sheets
into fuchsia pinks, petrol blues and scents that smell like our
    kitchen drawer,
Rubicon cartons stacked like dominoes,
gol gappeh to my right like yellow bubbles
too high for me to reach.

'*Jab ham java hongeh, janeh kaha hongeh,*' blares from
    loudspeakers,
cucumbers, tomatoes, *amrood* and juicy *aams* piled high,
hurri mircheh and tiny trees of *daniyah*.
A forklift stacks crates of Coke piled high to beamed ceilings,
pictures of turbaned men and korma on each spice box,
bags of flour with a tiger face on them follow me around.
'*Khabi kabhi, mereh dill meh*' plays on the speakers.

You take me to sticky *matai* counters.
'*Eh chokree! Iskoh haat na lagaa!*'
Juicy brown *gulaab jamans*, *jalebi* and *ladus*
with *sheerah* I want to suck off my fingers.

'Bangles!' I say, glittered glass hoops in sizes too small.
At the counter, he squeezes my hand tight to find my size.
I learn for the first time how easily the skin cuts and bleeds.

DRONE

A low hum in the air.

Soft feet in the night.
Your silhouette as you reach the door handle
enters.
Your snug body nestles into mine,
a hot water bottle to my stomach.
My arms wrap around you, anchor your fears
– how you warm me.

I bury my face in your hair.
Kiss the nape of your little neck, see the apple
of your left cheek rise.
Your hand, tiny, finds its way to mine.
They look like a new species of starfish.

The hum louder now.

'Did I whisper too loud, Mummy?'
'No, my darling, no.'
The windows start their death rattle.
You squeeze my hand harder, the whites of your eyes
grow, clutch me.
My arms try to anchor your fears.
'My baby, it's going to be OK.
Hush, it's going to be OK.
Don't cry, don't scream, I'm here,
I'm here, Mummy's here!'

The acrid smoke takes so long to clear.
'Celox, Celox, Celox, Celox!
Where's the Celox to help you clot?'
I hold your limp hand.
The starfish have sunk to the seabed.
Ears bleed; cold slices my skin, my muscles, takes grip
of my bones.

The screams I hear in the distance are my own.

PART I

MOTHER'S NATURE

You took your place in silence,
no idea what angels inscribed on you
burying yourself in the warmth of me.
Soon the soft tread of your tiny feet
left imprints within my belly;
what could possibly be closer?
Your hands stroked the water
rippling to make room for you.
When you sucked your thumb,
spun circles in the dark,
I soothed you to sleep –
no sense of night and day,
I became your time and you became
                              everything.

We conversed – Morse code,
tapping along my veins,
and your answers rang true in my mind.
Häagen-Dazs, cookies and cream,
Jacob's crackers and cream cheese,
vinegared chippy chips, not French fries
your dad had discovered at 2am, bleary-eyed.

When the pillars threatened to give way,
we held you in place through bed rest.
You stopped spinning, filled out,
pushing upwards.
I protested there was no more room.
You would stretch a limb as a reminder
that it was hard for you too.
Grinding your head against my bones,
you etched out your needs, perhaps to read back one day.
You needed more than this protection now.
You wanted others to hear our voice
and so the slow push of determination started.

You left clues along the way like hieroglyphic'd caves,

for those that would follow you in time.
And not even I expected you to emerge
as perfect as you did.
When the womb contracted, you heard her;
when I placed you against my breast,
you sighed –
we hadn't changed that much; now we would write on the
    outside.

Your feet would grow slower than your hands;
your tiny features I would marvel at,
that the small circle of your mouth
could make so much noise
as your glazed eyes started to focus on awe.

You soon grew along the length of my arm.
Your tight little fist gave way to unclammy palms
and you sprawled out asleep on your back,
unfurling the once-compact baby that was you.

Teeth fell out and I saved them as precious archives,
nappies to pull-ups to underwear,
crawling to walking to running
and still our silences spoke when our skin touched.

You made me a little box – told me to never open it,
in case the love you placed inside
escaped...

Four wheels switched to two and you were flying
over hills while sharp intakes of my breath
disappeared like smoke behind you.

Suddenly you were reading, asking millions of questions.
I felt proud when you started to answer them yourself,
teaching me what I struggled to catch up with.
You decided you didn't want to wear that top with those jeans,

wanted to discover the hours on the other side of daylight;
you said you knew he was the right one for you
and all the whispers arising from my bones said different.
I closed my mouth so they wouldn't shatter your dreams.
But they knew you,
for what could be closer?

When you turned up with wet hair and blackened eyes,
cradling all your mistakes in the cusp of your hand,
I made you walk upstairs,
leaving ash from simmering embers upon each stair
until all speckles of my ferocious anger at him
were but remnants – I refused to let it poison us.

We lay side by side, the lengths of my arms
measuring your experiences as I held you,
and once again our breathing slowed to sync,
we spoke no words.

Voices sang softly from an ancient ribcage,
soft tissues that once held you so close rose and fell.
Thoughts ran loop-like through our fingertips,
as clouds moved slowly across the vast sky.

We lay like this until the bones that had kept you upright
tapped ever so faintly against each other,
inscriptions you had once carved
explained what you now must do…

MY SON

I see you asleep, a sepia image: your plump soft face,
balled fists crossed tightly on your chest, protecting your
tiny heart.

A faint smile to try and make me feel better, the white
maggots around your body constantly moving. Kept at bay
by your beauty.

They won't harm you but won't let me touch you either.
I had a choice
and I…

Entombed in a glass paperweight, a red clot-like
flower I cannot touch yet carry with
me.

I WILL TELL GOD EVERYTHING

Ask if the lightning in the sky
was Him taking photos.
If not, I'll give Him my drawings.

The men with guns
and the aeroplanes of fire
will all get into trouble.

The sharp metal pieces
taken out of my stomach
will have to come with me.

I will tell God everything.
That Mama's face was gone
but I found Baba's feet
and put them together like shoes.

JASMINE

Scent of *motiyah* floats through thick smog, settles
near flickering red traffic lights.

How local beggars and rouged men in silken saris have ensnared them!
How, with barbed wire, they have pierced each flower's delicate hymen!
How the soft bracelets adorn their limp wrists,
wrists that flick matted heads!

Little girl not working fast enough, the corner of
Cavalry ground.
How her bangles rap against car windows,
not quite hard enough, not quite grabbing attention.
How she sings *pachas rupee baji, pachas rupee!*
Peering into me, as she leans towards the cavern of my car.

UNTITLED

The ground boiling, fumbling in darkness,
I peel myself off the bed –

lizards, cockroaches scarper.
I can hear you, bound and gagged –
the plot where you lie unclaimed.

Crickets among the remnants of wood fires,
the burnt edges of conscience.

Forgive me, sister, for taking my time.
I was only waiting for someone to name you.
Not as 'poor', neither 'Christian', nor as 'just a maid'.

                              *

I did pick you up gently,
cradling bone and body to my chest, warm as
when they left you there,
[violent ejaculation] from a shiny Audi,
[burnt] skin soothed by my fingertips,
[broken nose] restored by the palms of my hands,
[bloody] wiped with the edge of my *dupatta*.
I tried to straighten your fingers,
your blue lips –
re-plaited your oiled hair

                              *

I'm sorry, my sister, for taking my time.
At least now I can wrap you in white, scent you with camphor,
send you on your way with a name,
                    my dear sister
                                        Tahira

SREBRENICA – 11TH JULY

Today I speak.
Do you hear me?
Not in the tear of my dress
from the hem to the neck,
nor the clinks of the belts
leathering us together,
nor in the wail of the child left behind
to the tread of boots
trying to march to safety.

Do you see me?
Not in the burns on my flesh,
nor the bite marks on my breasts,
nor in the glints of glass
sitting in kidney trays
removed from wombs.

More than the names upon names
gathered in green boxes at the end of a page
or in pocketbook images of
clothes, berry-stained.

Do you think it's my cry you hear
from the šargija's hollow?
Caustic, strained, strange.
You won't find me
among the archives tallying the dead.

In the absence of our men we kept
home fires burning,
fought as best we could
when white eagles descended.

The kilns of the battlefield became our wombs instead.

Sedated, we ploughed through,
stomachs gnawing as men walked close by.

Bodies trembled at a glimpse of uniform
as we tried to stand upright and defy
the image of victim, the secret, the shame.

This was not our doing; it was done to us
as the world sang *never again.*

Voices rise
hoping someone will listen,
the tentative tongue
belonging to thousands of others
                    absent.
Will you ever hear them all?
Let their lives unfold a rich tapestry, now gone.
Can you see them lying among the forests now
scented with lilies?

Do you recognise this strength, my resilience, my name?
Do you know me?

TAP ON THE ROOF

The warning scud skirts the roof.

58 seconds to run

58 seconds to run

58 seconds to run

Slah Nuwasrah gathers his nephews,
Nidal wide-eyed.
Muhammad screams in his cot.
The pregnant wife frozen to her bed,
corner of the quilt chewed wet by clamped teeth.

48 seconds to run

48 seconds to run

48 seconds to run

Serrated edge of a warning phone call
spreads panic.
Hana frantically searches the yard.
'Where is Muhammad Malaka?'
Wheels of a little bike spin to a halt.

38 seconds to run

38 seconds to run

38 seconds to run

Basema sips her coffee,
thirsty from today's long fast.
Husband Mahmud has his feet up on the table – again.
She lovingly chides him and says, 'Don't, the children will do
    the same!'

28 seconds to run

28 seconds to run

28 seconds to run

Suha Abu Sada tries to force her legs to
move.
Clutches of her wheelchair mean she must stay put.
She stares out the window,
fingers circling prayer beads.

18 seconds to run

18 seconds to run

18 seconds to run

Argentina take on Holland.
Muhammed, Ibrahim, Salim, Suleiman, Musa, Hamdi
watch the penalties – laughing.

8 seconds to run

8 seconds to run

8 seconds to run

Naifa, eighty-two, cries remembering how once she would
    have sprinted,
sprinted down the three floors of her building,
cleared the hundred metres to a place where only her lungs
    would burn
from the acrid smoke.

7

    6

                5

        4

3

            2

                1

A small head amongst the garden, a house blown wide open
like a faceless corpse, just legs dangle from a mangled bike,
bloodied football shirts lying amongst the rubble, vultures on
high hilltops clapping – cawing at the show.

Operation Protective Edge.
58 seconds to run.

RACERS

barrel
bombs drop from above
                beginning their race
      olive branches gripped
like batons
           children

surely, a trouser rips
at the knee   a shoe comes
off   dresses tear apart at the
      seams –
sniper

fire from the rooftops
sparks at their heels, flames
in their hair
      bursts eardrums

flat lining   echoes
one boy's   golden smile
a two-finger   victory

      salute
      defiant   in his creaky
      wheelchair

CAMP EXILE

Morning and evening,
you will hear us maids cry,
Come buy our desert fruits!
Come buy, come buy!
Milkiest of limbs, the bluest eyes,
cheeks peach-blossomed;
taste them and try.
Plump unpicked cherries,
plucked at first spring,
smooth limbs, soft as honey – virgins,
full lips hidden by shy fingertips,
well worth the money that you'll bring!
Flowing locks, all colours cascading,
finest of them to set the pulse racing.

Laa tamshee, wa tat ruknee,
tafadhul wadhkhul la aindhee.
Don't walk past our makeshift homes.
Please, come in and see.
Today be my guest, detested, undress.
Your army boots, fatigues, suits, robes, *thobes* can rest
by the entrance.
You have never stayed long.
False promises of marriage, saviourship, love – all gone!

Lan tukalifuka katheerun – it won't cost you much.
Ask me how much it will cost you!
Just a morsel of bread for an impatient child.
When you tear my veils with yellowed fingers that probe,
Lan tukalifuka katheerun,
ask me how much it will cost you!
A pitcher of water for us to drink, that's all.
When you force yourself between my legs, I'll tell you,
Lan tukalifuka katheerun, iss alnee kam tukalifuk!
A blanket to cover us from the freeze of the night.
When you draw blood with your brutality, grip my hair so tight
I'll scream,

Lan tukalifuka katheerun, it won't cost you much,
iss alnee kam tukalifuk!
Clothes to cover my limbs from the wretched who abuse us.
When your sweat drips on me, your breath hot like panting
        beasts,
pushing my face into the grainy sands of a foreign land,
the sound of your grunting elation
making me want to burn you like fuel, for fuel,
Lan tukalifuka katheerun, iss alnee kam tukalifuk!
I'll tell you what it will cost you.

The backbones of each nation – the women who gave birth to
        the likes of you.
It will cost you the sisters you call your own,
those carrying all the injustices and burdens of war.
Ask me what this will cost you and I will tell you,
the daughters you once buried alive.
You learnt nothing from your saints and prophets.
It will cost you every Hawa, Asiyah, Mariam, Ayesha, Khadija.
It will cost you the women that you are so undeserving of,
once bearers of your children,
oh goblin men of no faith!

Your misogyny will choke you with
its own bitter fruits,
its poison carrying the rot of your existence to its death.
And the gaze on my daughter will one day be averted,
innocent eyes marked by the governments who abandoned,
tortured, raped and displaced us.

She who stands small in the corner, watching.
She who will move forward through this history of hurt.
She who will resolve to survive, rise.
She who will not be bought.
She who will not be sold.
She who will not be used,
will not be devoured,

chewed by the false humanity you offer.
Don't even look at her!
She will rise, one day, and defy
you.
Her name – *Syria*.

GULSHAN-E-IQBAL PARK

Yesterday in Sadar Mandi, next to the *sabzi-vala*'s wooden
    handcart,
you opened my passenger side door and took a seat,
de-creased the front of your brown starched *kameez* over your
    knees
like, maybe, your father used to,
and demanded I drive you to Anarkali as if you knew me.

I wonder now how many protests you stifled
at the sight of a lapel, peeled back
to reveal tightly assembled explosives
strapped to upper torso like an iron swaddle
before my car became your vehicle of choice.

We drove to three locations,
my pleas unable to cool the flame of your eyes,
your face – a scream
when you couldn't decide
where to deliver your hatred.

You slammed my car door as you left.

Today the swings in Gulshan-e-Iqbal Park are cracked red,
the chains charred and redundant.
The overturned choo-choo train simmers
like, maybe, your heart used to,
while a footless shoe joins the pile of empties at the side
gates.

You found your way.

LAHORE

Yes, you're too noble to glance down at your well-groomed feet,
devoid of any fear about a deity you might one day meet.
Yes, your flash cars whisk you away from all this poverty.
If you close your eyes tight enough, you won't have to see
the old man before you that you dismiss so easily.

His mustard tattered clothes, no shoes on dirty feet,
struggling to gather money so his family can eat.
His small creased eyes – the anguish of making ends meet.
His mouth utters supplication upon supplication for me
even though I tell him I have nothing to give.
'I'd never talk to strangers if I wasn't *majboor*
but, *bebe*, I am a poor man with hands outstretched.'

The white of his long beard and cream-turbaned head,
skin tanned and wrinkly covering a body – unfed.
He tries to talk to two youths parked next to me.
They brush him aside, pretending to be deaf purposely,
eyes suddenly blinded to him, faces dead proud.
Why converse with a man who fails to fit in with the crowd?
Life's about pleasure, indulging in merriment.
Why give a shit when you lie in bed – content?

The old man disappears into enveloping thin air.
The two youths don't realise to what extent they've been unfair.
An ample opportunity missed,
small act of kindness for a cycle of bliss.

Imagine a day of reckoning – a mountain of good deeds
and as you're accounted, those deeds disappear quickly
till, at the very end, the man you so easily now ignored
becomes the most valuable asset to help settle your score.

He won't be the valueless poor beggar then, will he?
You won't comprehend his tattered clothes and his feet so dirty.
The same white beard, warm eyes, you won't now be ignoring,
and he'll smile a knowing smile, watching your hands

        outstretched
– begging.

At last my mother returns, a weighty purse in cupped hands,
and I frantically search the crowd for that desperate old man.
He cries and then smiles at the thought that I would bring
a gift for him, '*Bebe*, I'll remember you on the day of
reckoning.'

PART II

THERE IS NO SUCH THING AS ISLAMOPHOBIA

You should have seen how I took her down,
pulled that towel right off her head in town.
She was screaming as I spat in her face.
These rag-heads taking over all our space.
I'll teach her to go back to where she comes from…

There is no such thing as Islamophobia!

Settle down, settle down, boys, bell went ages ago!
Now, in light of recent events, let's discuss Charlie Hebdo
I think Prophet Mohammed T-shirts should be worn to
    challenge offended Muslims everywhere.
And every other schoolkid turns to the one Muslim boy and
    stares,
the same stare he gives back
when slapped
by older schoolboys, who tell him
he's a Paki terrorist.

There is no such thing as Islamophobia!

It's hot on this damn tube
in my smart shoes and business suit
and I'm seeing this hummus-eating, camel-shagging Paki
    Muslim slut
and I turn to Greg next to me and say I don't give a fuck.
My freedom of speech gives me the choice,
so I sing at the top of my voice,
Kill them, kill them all…

There is no such thing as Islamophobia!

The sun bears down on an Essex park,
lighting up crisp blades of grass.
A breeze moves gently through flowers of red
where a woman in a burkha and scarf lies dead.
Sixteen stab wounds decorated her body, they said…

There is no such thing as Islamophobia!

I didn't need to run up fast.
That old Muzzrat just shuffled past.
Three quick stab wounds to his back.
Went down instantly in the attack.
Planted bombs at his nearby masjid.
Tipton, Walsall, you get my drift.
'Self-starter' racist I am, not a terrorist!

There is no such thing as Islamophobia!

There are two exits to Grimsby mosque
but we had each one boxed off.
A petrol bomb for each one
and one for the roof, job done.
For queen and country we served well,
ex-soldiers if you couldn't tell.
We're patriotic, us, not extreme.
We're just trying to keep Britain clean.

There is no such thing as Islamophobia!

Status: *Obviously when I got on the plane I checked no one looked like a terrorist*
Status: *Mate I changed tube cos a bearded man sat there reading arabic scripture muttering under his breath*
Status: *Dunno what the hell they carrying under their veils – I ain't getting killed for political correctness*
Status: *Why do your people hate our West so much that you wanna destroy it? Piss off back to where you came from*
Status: *For every person beheaded by these sick savages we should drag 10 off the streets and behead them, film it and put it online. For every child they cut in half… we cut one of their children in half. An eye for an eye mate*

There is no such thing as Islamophobia!

Daily Mail – Muslims tell us how to run our schools.
The Independent – Fundamentalists plotting to bring jihad
    into the classrooms.
Daily Star – Muslim sickos – Maddie kidnap shock.
Daily Express – Hogwash, now the PC brigade bans piggy
    banks in case they offend Muslims.
The Sun – Muslim convert beheads woman.
Evening Standard – Muslim plot to behead soldier in UK.
Brit kids forced to eat halal school dinners.
Al Qaeda Corrie threat.
Jihadist plot to take over city schools.
Ramadan a ding-dong.
Halal secret of Pizza Express.
Muslim thugs are just 12 in knife attack on Brit schoolboy.
Muslims loonies hijack elections.
Muslim-only loos.
Muslims
Muslims
Muslims

There is no such thing as Islamophobia…

CUTS OF THE CLOTH

The cloth, the fabric, the outer garb
Stitch together power and class,
Needles of culture piercing holes
Into cuts of cloth, dyed, tenfold,
Used to impress ideologies on me,
Binding beliefs when I want to be free.

The cloth, the fabric, the outer garb
Robed kings, emperors, pharaohs past,
Bred disdain and prejudice towards those in rags
Though it all shrouds the same as body-bags.

The cloth, the fabric, the outer garb
Draped over coffins of soldiers who guard,
Foreign policies sewn into coats of arms
Worn with pride though it fails to save them from harm.

And the flag, that colourful cloth fixates courses
Of destruction to pillage a country's resources
Under the rhetoric of setting veiled women free,
But last time I checked, no one asked me

If the cloth, the fabric, the outer garb
Restricted my freedom or caused me harm.
Who decides if I want to be liberated of this
Or whether making myself naked will give me bliss?

My covering veils me, protects me, my sacred way of life.
Your army fatigues help you blend in and cause strife.
Do you think you're winning hearts and setting nations free
Or breeding resentment throughout vast family trees?
They too will bury their young under differing nation colours.
Strip them all back and we're all sisters and brothers,
Cut from the same cloth, soaked in different dyes.
We could connect on many levels if we eradicate the lies.

The cloth, the fabric, the outer garb
Have long served me with their liberating charm
Of allowing control of who sees me, who doesn't.
I never ordered or demanded or ever summoned
You – when silk stockings were what governed
Your moods, but I'm backward and you're modern,
While behind institutional doors you continue to play,
Latex and rubber keeping your hypocrisy at bay.

The cloth, the fabric, the outer garb
Become banners through which revolutions are charged.
They can be markers of injustice and oppression at large,
Orange jumpsuits and hooded inmates not yet discharged,
Yet the cloth covering my face causes you alarm?

Breaches security, you say, and has no significance,
Causing you to maintain from me a safe distance,
But this cloth defies you and becomes my resistance,
For what good is freedom if you deny my existence?
The cloth, the fabric, the outer garb
Speaks for me, my thoughts and what's in my heart…

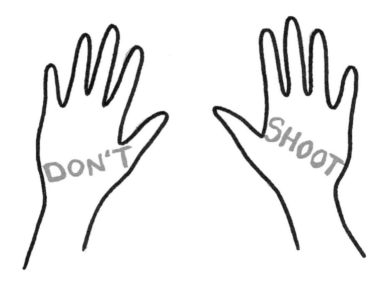

I CAN'T BREATHE

Did Fanon know, so many years ago,
that this world would be ablaze with fire
when he stated, 'We revolt simply because,
for many reasons, we can no longer breathe'?

Did he know that the bones
of the people of colour like gunpowder
would ignite skies garnering places like Ferguson,
Missouri, Manhattan, New York, Washington and Boston
together in peaceful protests chanting,
'I can't breathe'?

Could he have known the last words each young black man
   would whisper,
Michael Brown, eighteen, saying,
'Stop shooting, I don't have a gun'?
Could he have heard Trayvon Martin, seventeen, say,
'What you following me for?' before Zimmerman's nine-
   millimetre pistol went off?
Did Fanon hear the echo of fifty bullets blast twenty-three-
   year-old Sean Bell
as he told his best friend he loved him too?
Did he hear Kendrec McDade, nineteen, ask the officers, 'Why
   did you shoot me?' on the back of a lie that he was armed,
or could he have known that a police officer would
   accidentally pull out his gun instead of a Taser
and shoot Oscar Grant, twenty-two, in the back,
and later
would he have known that John Crawford's mother would hear
   her twenty-two-year-old son screaming,
'It's not real!' on the phone – shot for holding a pellet gun in
   Walmart, Ohio?
Or Amadou Diallo, a shy twenty-three-year-old brother shot
   forty-one times for pulling out a wallet?
Did he hear seven-year-old Aiyana Stanley-Jones, in Detroit,
   shot on her sofa when she said…?

She was sleeping.

We are bleeding.

Deadly policies of anti-black racism.
See, they say Eric Garner was a big man,
asthmatic.
And that's why the chokehold killed him.

Bullshit.

They say he was selling untaxed cigarettes
and that's why
they're justified
for the seatbelt hold
that caused him to say,
eleven times,
'I can't breathe.'

Like Middle Passage swallowed souls
in oceans deep,
these streets have swallowed yours,
but we keep memories alive – our children will feel your
    presence,
mothers will make sure they soak up your essence
and demand the change your demise must inspire,
or we lose hope and they gain
and nothing will change.

We are breathing.

Our existence is not just the earth,
nor the streets, the barrels of guns or the deceased.
Our earth is our minds.
Where we find, where we find, where we find –
our healing.

We will not become those who hurt us,
will not become those who fear us,
not become those who deny us,
defy us, revile us.
Change is coming.

Breathe.

PART III

TOW TRUCKER

Khatam hogaya, you say,
explaining why the gasket's blown.
The word 'master' in black
glistens on the truck.

Grimy Airtex top with a police badge on your slim chest,
fingers that bend deftly all the way back,
dirty with oil and grime.

I bet the tip of that thumb touches the wrist.
Ears stick out a little,
hair oily, slicked down.
I wonder as you lean against the car
whether you remove your armpit hair.

Oh, I seen you looking,
just before you climb into your tow truck.
Sneaking a little glance,
then a long look through your rear mirror,
then your wing mirror
across a bony shoulder,

catch my eye.

I wonder who's given you the silver ring you wear.
She's lucky.
Your new beard will never rough up her skin.

TO YOU

Lingering cigarette smoke,
our discarded shoes point
in different directions.

The blue mug brewing yesterday's tea
on the worktop
and the teaspoon you said takes the heat away.

The disfigured toothbrush,
your broken watch with its cruel hands
that stare intently.

God told us we are like garments to one another,
so today I am wearing six of your tops,
carrying all of you with me,
like the time you lifted me and my muddy wellies
out of that ditch.

I need to tell you
that the heavy rug has moved, that paint stain
you caused when we decorated
peeps at me like a great aubergine eye.
I sit on different sofas and watch it cry.

Oh, and the bed still smells of your scent.

I have decided to keep it that way,
half-expecting to hear your faint snores,
see your rising shape under the covers

and the whisper,
Inna lillahi wa inna ilayhi raajioon.

THE ARGUMENT

The moonlit tarmac has constricted,
as narrow as the heart beneath this breastbone.
Cars precariously balance on uneven pavements
like novice skaters blading on ice.
'Speak!' you retort.

I barely hear you, but the spinster down the road
turns her head swiftly
and the leafman perched on the wall to my left
nimbly crosses his legs and grins.

'Speak to me!' you bellow,
and the old school bars pierce through grass and grit.
Black spears behind your head – nothing is safe any more.
Two empty crisp bags – silver eyes, human-height apart –
watch intently across the road

'Why won't you talk to me?'
The leafman grins from the wall, wrings his hands; claps
and teardrops form a language no one understands

I jump as you shout, 'Is this what we've come to?'
You've grown fangs – glisten through your beard like icicles,
your half-shadowed face
as you finally whisper desperation.

'Why won't you speak to me?'
I want to say I was trying to remember
the digits of a long-forgotten number,
but – like you – I hear nothing.

SADDLEWORTH

So here we are,
you driving me through the narrowest country lanes.
Even the tarmac spreads herself out at speed for you.

Outside – willow trees stoop as they see you coming;
inside – fickle words settle at my boots like blossom.
'The window cleaner lives on the right,'
you say, and
this is how you rectify our demise.

I know what you're trying to do,
buying love with a French chef and three rosettes,
as if I'll pin them right through to the skin of my breast.

A prized possession; I look away or this body will offer itself,
drown out whispers from bones seeped in love.
It's getting dark as hilltops rise watching our headlights.

If I sleep early tonight, I think the world will keep spinning.

EPIPHANY

Göteborg, along the A27.
An immaculate service-station toilet
near Kroksjön's Fish Camp, to be precise.

Pants still down by my ankles,
he declares, 'In the third of the night, you
will find what you need with your Lord –

                                    pray!'

CYCLES

charred arteries, the trees
almost touching
the moon, its cycle and mine
　　　passing
　　　us by

each time I bleed, trying to warn
you,
never let it be said I did not tell
　　　you of your
　　　neglect

did not listen to
each other's
　　　breathing
to hear who sleeps first

the moon still lights the chasm
between us,
too close and it will swallow
　　　us whole

BUNTING

I watch, through the window, the digital
clock, each second sluggish,
refusing to acknowledge the train
just about to

leave. Between us the air hardens – the table our
referee; if it had arms
it would be pushing a hand into our chests.

Earlier, outside the station,
bunting the colour of pulped fruit
struggled to release itself,
the string not letting the flags blow
free:

      little shark's teeth
spread over three rows. If they had
a voice they'd be screaming:
Let me go, let me

               go!

TEASPOONS

Today, you kissed me passionately,
a welcome change from the pat
on my head, reward for the hoovering
and stack of ironed clothes –

not enough, though, for a transaction of lovemaking.

Maybe, if I cook your favourite tea,
warm the plates or separate
all the plastics from the rubbish,

would you stroke my hair / place your hand
gently in the small of my back / gaze into
my eyes / perhaps lean towards me and give
                    more than a

                                    teaspoon?

PRISM

Aligning my legs like lines of coke, you –
seek pleasure as I watch,
cut the atmosphere – myriad colours,
a prism in which I entomb myself –

you –

STRANGEWAYS

A woman's infidelity affects a man:
the cell walls constrict,
> bulging eyes,
> vein bulbous as it throbs at the side of the head –
fists pounding concrete,
metal bars watching a grown man cry.

He pulls her suspenders around her throat
tight, to the clang
> of the warden's keys every night,
> forgiving her only as the echo disappears.

No one noticed
the pool of crimson glistening at the foot of his chair.

They say it was love
that taped the rusty blade to his toothbrush,
> mercy that left
> > the deep lines strafing his arms.

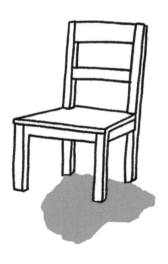

DERELICT HOUSES

A leak through the ceiling.

A naked woman, still
lips, stapled zip-like.

A man has abandoned her.

Another, crouched beneath the table,
cradles a baby in cupped hands.

A contorted man pinned to the corner
tries to buckle his jacket straight.

All are orange and mud-green,
colours that no one chooses.

They splatter everything,
rust creeping up their legs like a bright disease.

All of them empty, all of them leaking.

WHEN SHE LEFT

Our egg chairs face each other in the garden
like broken headphones

still

I wait for sound…

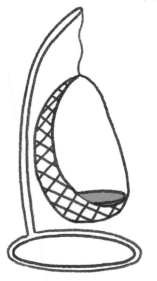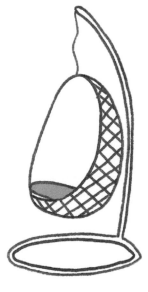

BLISS

Oh and surely it comes,
   waves upon waves,
back and forth,
   wind in hair, sea salt on lips,
sky dark and shore on fire,
   sun just about to set,
breath poised,
   every atom in its place.

White-frothed waves swallow sand – crescendo all-powerful.

We all stand still
   catching our breath,
drinking up the sea.
   Resting outstretched,
dissolve into the night,
   swirls of wind plucking us up.
Different measures of pleasure –
   this is bliss…

I AM

The ray of dusty sunlight sneaking through the blinds in the morning, I have woken you.

The sudden scent of jasmine among the fumes of diesel and I have made you turn your head.

The colour of the neon scarf swept by the wind into littered streets is how I caught your eye.

Heartbeat quickens and the blush of heat across your face as you fight to deny my existence, you can but try.

Lemon scent lingering on your fingers as you crush my leaves, you can only wash me off.

Flecks of diamonds glinting across the lakes prompt you to blink me away, you put on your shades.

The hot wet kisses of lust sacrificed at the altar in the night are futile, you can't hide from me.

The flutter in the womb as the packed limbs move helps me start to open the delicate bud of your heart.

I am the discarded silky cocoons of the butterflies,

the darkest stain of sappanwood in the bowels of moored ships.

I am the fodder of golden cattle grazing among the dead,

the morning dew hidden among the leaves of dense forests.

I am the richness you cannot see when counting coins.

I run through your veins when all has dried and withered.

I am what you wanted me to be and I'm here.

The ray of dusty sunlight sneaking through the blinds in the morning, I have woken you.

JIMMY, JIMMY, JIMMY

I catch you one night: high-vis uniform,
flat cap shining as the ticket prints,
and run up, flustered, to my car,
ask why you did that.

Startled, you stare, lowering your machine.
'If I'd known it was you, I wouldn't have given
the ticket, but I've punched it through now!'

You look like a tired disco dancer,
red weary eyes, gold chain winking at your neck.
I ask for your name and you say Jimmy.
'No! Your real name.'

'Amrit Laal from Gujarat,' you tell me,
And I admit, like a long-abandoned friend,
'Sometimes I call myself Annie. And we came
from India too, before '47, a place called Sunam!'

Our bastardisation rears like a welt from a colonial whip.

An old familiarity embraces us. 'I'm sorry.
If I'd known…' We exchange a wave
as if we have had many goodbyes, not quite like siblings
or lovers, but maybe friends from a different life.

FORD DAGENHAM, 1984

Trays of red roast chicken
Carried by your ox-like hands
Into your workplace.

Red roast chicken – an offering.
Red roast chicken – to sway

John, who calls you a Paki
To your face on the assembly line.
For Brian, who complains
You get all the night shifts.

Red roast chicken – an offering.
Red roast chicken – a bribe

For Arun and Gurinder, who sit
In the pub with the Johns and the Brians,
Planning how to disrupt
The speed of your assembly line.

Red roast chicken – an offering.
Red roast chicken – to sway

Tommy, who cracks the glass
Of each car door on its way to you.
You have only thirty seconds to check
And each faulty one is less pay for you.

Your ox-like hands work quickly,
The same ox-like hands that beat
The chicken pieces tender, spiced
And marinated them all the night before.

You watch all those who do not care
To know your name
Eat the red roast chicken carried by you
Into your workplace.

ONYX I

He came to my garden door,
A robin between his teeth.
I didn't let him in
Until he put the bird down

She flew off, orange chest fiery.
My God, she flew.

Yesterday I saw her perched on the fence.
She came to say hello,
The black bird
Keeping watch on another fence,
Majestic, puffing his chest out,
Guarding his territory,
Marvelling at her.

Today
I buried her headless torso,
Onyx side-eyeing her, then
yawning to look away.

ONYX II

Moribund, she uttered.
A stethoscope cuffed the vet's neck.
I, virgin to this word,

Cradled Onyx's head,
Sleek fur sloughing my hands.
As breath raptured

In gasps, a syringe of yellow liquid
Rolled marble eyes backwards.
I folded into the curves of warm limb,
Was not sure who kept who warm,
As I stood by the sink, cleaning his face
With soft towels, removing cannulas,

Wrapping him in white,
Lowering him into damp soil,
Knee-deep as if burying us both.

Now his sister mourns,
Shedding her hair, as she traces him
To the mound in our garden.

RANI

Tonight I walked in and you greeted me as your sister,
kissed my hands as if I crossed oceans to be here.
You recited Persian poetry, your eloquent English buried now,
speaking to nurses only in Urdu while they ticked sheets,
    pretending to understand.

Tonight I walked in and you greeted me as a single woman,
asked me if I'm married, or if I wanted the cup of tea
you think you brewed a while ago standing in your kitchen,
your fisted boned hands tight like clamshells on sandy pillows.

Tonight I walked in and you thought I'm your granddaughter's
    friend.
Asked if my university is far and whether I ate almonds to help
    me study.
You insisted I take down the clothes you think you washed today
as I unfurled the curling question mark your body has become.

Tonight I walked in and…

Your apology on loop – *'Sorry meh bhoolgayee,*
merah koy nay heh – jiskah koy nay hotah, uskah khuda hota heh'
    – the film *Sholay*?
You recreate my blood line every day.
'Aap koh pata heh? You are Nazia,
your brothers are Farooq and Aftab.'
Lodgers living in our house
forty years ago.

You still think Sufyan is fourteen,
insist at six o'clock to make *roti* for your husband,
shout to whoever's listening,
'Wake my mother up!' – she died five years ago.
Persian couplets leave your lips and I can't understand you again.

'*Haaji paaji sharabi!*' you recite when agitated.
Your husband props up your pillow,
hoists you a little upright to stop you disappearing under the
white shroud.
He chews the delicate flesh of an apple between his teeth,
and places it in your mouth as if you're Eve.

ALU PARATAH

My son, wide-eyed and curious,
Stands near the kitchen stove,
A smoky *tawa* spitting till piping hot,
Ready to bake thin potato-filled *parateh*.

He stares at his dadi-jaan's asbestos hands,
Used to the heat, tirelessly providing,
Places his hands on her shoulders
And says, 'Teach me to make an *alu paratah*!'

From my prayer mat in the dining room
I hear her dish up firm words of advice,
'It's a woman's job to cook and a man's to earn,'
And the slow licking of fire starts its slow burn.

'While I'm alive,' she says, 'I'll make them,
And when I don't, your mother will,
And when she can't, your wife will,'
Her beliefs as perfect as her round *parateh*.

NANI AND THE WASHING MACHINE

A regal woman with shy glints of gold,
she kindles fires within her chest.
The glimpse of her silvery red hair from beneath her *chadar*
defies her eighty-eight years.
Life has inscribed stories amongst her wrinkled skin.
Softened with scented oils, her touch is smooth.
But the mind still sharp wrestles with signs,
wrestling with the dials and symbols
of a machine with no instruction.
Cycles of thoughts spinning with the drum
for three hours now.

No one to explain, she calls out for the imaginary children
who have left only their shadows behind.
She tugs at the clip, trying to open the door,
but the door remains locked.
The days of dhobis with stones and water have gone.
Voiceless boxes with wires in their place, confusing her,
defying her intellect once enriched with pistachios and almonds,
nurtured with love, *ghee*, fresh *saag*, *kishmish* and *makhan*.

She can still work out your monthly costs,
recall every incident of pain you told her,
recite ayahs of the Quran from memory,
make a *roaster salan* like no other,
but today, the cycle of the washing machine
reminds her of inadequacies,
a body that cannot stride continents to be with loved ones,
of fingers that don't FaceTime without help,
of an old lady who cannot guard her handbag while shopping,
of a woman who fails to stop a cycle from spoiling her clothes
for three hours now.

She is nothing but days.
The drum of the machine still spins.
She thinks the dust of the earth as her blanket,
wanting to see her great-grandchildren marry

before she's lowered into her place of rest,
but she can't stop her clothes from spoiling.

Three long hours now and counting.

SONGS OF PROTEST

The first form of protest I ever saw
was in a gathering of women,
conservative, strict, steadfast,
all leaving the layers accumulated over time at the door.
Slow careful unravelling of headscarves
unveiling shy glints of tinder beneath black robes.

In the centre of the room
a hollowed drum, leathered skin tight on either end,
a silver baton-like spoon tapping surely against it,
bangled hands clapping, no placard in sight,
only the familiar glint of fire in the eyes,
the tell-tale sign when women have had enough.
The strictest of them dipped the shoulder to give permission,
and women morphed to megaphones.

Sueh ve cheeray valia meh kendiyah
Kar chatree di chaawm cha meh bendiyah

Each recalling her love, her heartache, her joy, her hopes,
laughter pulsating the room, women – heads back, chest
    defiant,
firm hands on each other's shoulders.
Allies sat tight-knit together, knee to knee in solidarity,
no one to silence this protest as they sang,

Kala doriyah kundeh naal ariyeh oi chotah devra pabbi na
    laraya oi
Kukri oh lendi jeri kur kur kardi eh, soreh nay jan, sus bur bur
    kar dee heh
Kala doriyah kundeh naal ariyeh oi chotah devra pabbi na
laraya oi

Women roaring against injustice
through words, through beats, through song
challenging those accusing them of being wrong,
hands on hip, fingers pointing at the imaginary accused,

practice against oppressors absent from the room.
One by one they rose, fists as microphone.

Teri maa nekpakaya andeh, Asi mangeya tah pehgay dandeh
Lateh di chadar uteh salethi rang maya
Aavoh saamneh aavoh samneh kolo deh ruskeh na lung maya

My first lesson speaking out against injustice
as each generation ignored their knees quaking,
voices shaking, defiant against men weaponising our silence,
all the matriarchs raising their heads high
looking out for the silent ones, the timid ones,
their flick of the hand across the room as they caught our eye
a signal to us fledglings to sing,

Hoh rang barseh bheegi chunar vali rang barseh, hoh rang
barseh bheegi chunar vali rang burseh

Meanings did not matter to us,
we the generation of women who flit between identities,
the partitioned ones, the fragmented ones,
never seen as the whole ones.
The old ones with the new ones, the traditional ones with the
modern ones,
the singing ones with the unheard ones,
the Pakistani ones with the British ones.

Balle balle, bai torr punjaban di, balle balle bai torr
punjaban di,
Jutti khall di marorra nahion chal di,
Torr punjaban di , balle balle

Meanings did not matter to us.
Our gatherings helped the hymens of our voices break into
song.
The first lesson – communication of our struggles,
each chorus in unison.

Second lesson – unity of our protest,
each generation holding the hands of the next.
Third lesson – have strength and courage while doing so,
knee bent proudly for our cause.

Mathay te chamkan vaal, mereh banreh deh,
Lao ni lau ennu shagna'n di mehndi,
Lao ni lau ennu shagna'n di mehndi,
Mehndi karreh hath laal, mereh banreh deh

Years later, when we questioned our ability to love, to be loved,
to have love, to touch love,
questioned our permission to surround ourselves with love,
questioned the desire to entertain love,
questioned our denial to love,
followed our fiery steely-hard determination to find and
        become that love,
the songs of our women rang in our ears.

Chittah kukkar a banareh deh, qaasni dubbateh valiyeh,
        mundah sadkeh teerh teh...

OUTRO

BROWN BODIES

Authu billahi minashaytan nirajeem, bismillah hirah mah
   niraheem.

Where I come from, we begin by warding off the devil first,
then praise the Lord's name, Most Merciful, Most Gracious.

Alhamdulillahi rabbil alameen, arahmah niraheem, maliki
   yawmideen, iyya ka nabadu wa iyya ka nastaeen.

I pray for guidance, for lordship, for mercy.

Ihdinasaratul mustakeem, siratuladheena, anamta alayhim,
   ghayril maghdubi alayhim waladua aleeen, ameen.

The Opener, verses that are mother to our holy book,
a cure, the key, a foundation for seekers of truth,

seven repeated verses, five times a day,
and yet man has learnt to twist my Lord's word for power.

By the orange glow of burning bushes
I have seen altars in alternate worlds
where brown girls swathed in white cotton
are led to lie on concrete slabs, for sacrifice.

In this absence of divine decrees and cracked moon miracles
an abundance of misguided men
sacrificing women in the name of false gods.
Candles lit by men around these women
to ensure people see the darkness they bring.
Women who uttered those wretched words of sin,
that blasphemous declaration – 'My life is my own.'

Where I come from, brown girls are offered up
ek dum, in one breath, *ek dum*, in a moment of time, *ek dum*,
to idols of fear, expectation, duty and selflessness,
always becoming less of self to attain purity.
Always through the guise of love are we held to obey,

told to suffer this pain in order to make it to heaven's door.
They say that's the only way to please the Lord.

'Be patient, it's better to let the skin keep score.
Bawl, scar, cut, cry, bleed,
but not so other people can see.
Hide your sorrow, mask your despair.
Don't complain within earshot of anyone; others will hear.
Don't look like you're falling apart.
If you don't find the God in you, it'll be the devil in your heart.'

But I am falling apart
like I can't breathe,
a fresh hangman's knot formed in the lynch ground of my gut
    each day,
we the women who fear the deaths of our hearts
more than the deaths of our bodies.

In my world, planets stop and slowly orbit in opposite
    direction and everything feels wrong.

How we're indoctrinated to believe
it's the woman, always, who must bow down,
to adapt, to appease, to silence herself in the grand scheme of
    things.
'This is our way,' they say, 'how it's always been.'

We, the investments – the 'value' on honour,
performing for people our parents always talk about.
'Beta – log kiya kayngeh?'

You always worried what the people would say.

We, the retirement plans of in-laws.
We, the bodies pounded by misogyny and female toxicity.
We, only as pure as our sacred vaginas.

We, judged for the veiling or the unveiling of our bodies.
We, our worth measured only in relation to others,
so when we are finally on our own
we're left to wonder what it is we amount to.

'Just keep cooking the things he loves.
He gives you money, doesn't he?
Big house, a fancy car, all of the above.'

I've been trying to tell you all
that we aren't as close any more.

'Don't bleed on the tablecloth, go cry elsewhere.
If you're religious enough, depression won't affect you, dear!'

But I don't want to stay in a marriage where I can't be myself.
Each day the weight crushes chest bone
to powder, till this heart has no covering at all.
I've told you – I'm not doing this any more!

'Think of the kids, dear, don't be naïve – concentrate.
Who will ever marry them if you separate?
Be positive, remember God, you're in a better position than
        others.
Stop with these heathen thoughts and busy yourself with zikr.'

Where I come from, scaffoldings of support,
a spider's silk web.
One gust of strength – quickly nothing left.
Soon, fossilised women curled up foetus-like emerge
in battered leather suitcases buried deep beneath the earth.
Saba Qaiser – one shot to the head,
a gunny bag as shroud, dumped along a riverbed.
My sisters, Banaz Mahmod and Qandeel Baloch,
Shafilea Ahmed and Samia Shahid,
Rania Alayed and Samaira Nazir,

Khalida Bibi and Samia Sarwar,
Ghazala Khan and Sadia Sheikh,
Farzana Parveen and Rukhsanah Naz,
Saira Rani and Sabeen Thandi,
Farkhunda Malikzada, whose name meant 'to prosper'.

These women sacrificed to false gods I do not recognise,
courageous women, who had said, 'My life is mine!'
Challenging patriarchy – always fucking patriarchy,
the kind of patriarchy not limited by colour,
injustices inflicted by men with power.

Courage is standing up to propagators of shame.
Courage is challenging man-made notions of honour.
Courage is knowing that women die for speaking their truth.

Cursed be the red-eyed demons reading
my beloved Lord's decree backwards.

These sisters all made to step backwards,
robbed of stepping into the lives they'd yearned for.
My God is not unjust, I whisper.
My God is not unjust, I say.
My God is not unjust, I scream.

Who the fuck are you worshipping?

Two minutes to midnight, New Year's Eve,
stood alone in the dark of my garden.
I gather the bones of my spine and stand tall,
learning that the capacity to be alone
is the capacity to love, with no conditions,
no possession, no addiction, no reliance,
allowing others absolute freedom, letting no one harness
      yours.
I must teach those around me
that things are going to be different now.

*Fa inna ma al usree yusra, fa inna ma al usree yusra, fa inna ma
    al usree yusra.*

The sky is a furnace of raging colour
and I know in my bones that it celebrates for me.
Ablaze in the hope of new beginnings,
it's so close I can touch it.

No more will I exile myself from myself.
I'm ready. 'My life is my own.'

ACKNOWLEDGEMENTS

Above all, Alhamdulillah for everything.

For all my people, past and present, who believed in me and my words, I will always be in gratitude to each and every one of you.

Thank you…

To my Nani, my mum & dad, my siblings Sham Z, Faizan I, Ray B and Shamas R, Naz & Sarah, Romana M, Uncle Bobby, all my treasured nieces & nephews, family and friends – those who supported me along my journey, notably Naveed B, Mariyah B, Idreece B, Ismaeel B, Isshaaq B, Ilyaas B, Ammaarah R, Shaheena A, Nabiha M, Alex G, Pakeezah Z, Yasmin B, Zoltan H, Nikki M, Adie N, Elmi A, Yusra W, Saria K, Nasima B, Sarah Y, Carla H, Mahboobeh R, Omenah R, Arash S, Usma M, Ahmed M, Ummi F, Nureen A, Aisha M, Shahid I, Ali I, Amna A, Nuradin A, Kalpa V, Afshan D, Shaguftah I, Shemiza R, Manchester Muslim Writers' Zahid Hussain, Future's Venture's Keisha T, Alison S, poets who inspired and/or encouraged me – Salena Godden, Sabrina Mahfouz, Mimi Khalvati, Caroline Bird, Jackie Kay, Jack Underwood, Helen Mort, Danez Smith, Kaveh Akbar, Andrew McMillan, Chris Jam, SuAndi, Shamshad Khan, Warsan Shire, STAND Magazine's Jon & Elaine Glover & John Whale, The Poetry Exchange's John Prebble, Fiona Lesley, Commonword's Martin De Mello, Pete Kalu, Nadeem Z, Fereshteh M, Women in the Spotlight's Charlotte M, Jane B, Bethany H, Christina F, Deborah C, Sui A, Heena C, Yolanda M, Col B, Dipali D, Shahireh S, Naomi S, In Place of War's Ruth Daniel, PANDA Arts' Ann-Marie, Manchester Literature Festival's Sarah-Jane Roberts, the Apna's Arry Nessa, Three Minute Theatre's Gina & John, NCA's Peter Wells ,Manchester International Festival's Dan & Julie, Jerwood Fellows Amy L, Simon B, Erinma O & Chanje K, TOAST's Lewis Buxton & all fellow TOAST 2016 poets like Laurie B, MMU's

Jacqueline R, all my amazing fellow team members on the Artistic Directors Leadership Programme, Anjum A, Summayya S, Sadiah S, Nasreen R, Farheen A, Tasnim A, Madhu P, Sima S, Shirin B, Joanna B, Bryn M, Leyla H, Sadia H, Hodan Y, Saju A, Rana K, Kasia N, Azeezat J, my anchors Angela K, Sarah D & Anne S and of course Burning Eye Books' Clive, Bridget, Liv & Harriet for making this happen!

A Note on the Cover Photography:

GETTING TO THE HEART OF THE PROBLEM

When we're injured, blood clots are life-savers, preventing us from losing too much blood. However, when blood clots form unnecessarily inside blood vessels, they can be deadly. Each year in the UK around 100 000 people die from cardiovascular diseases like heart attack or stroke caused by unwanted blood clots. This image shows red blood cells captured in the net-like fibres of a blood clot, one of which has been compressed into a heart shape by the contracting fibres. Image author Fraser Macrae at the University of Leeds, is using state-of-the-art methods to study the structure of blood clots in patients with cardiovascular disease and how the differ to clots in healthy people.

Fraser Macrae, University of Leeds.